Bus Driver

Laura K. Murray

seedlings

CREATIVE EDUCATION • CREATIVE PAPERBACKS

Published by Creative Education and Creative Paperbacks
P.O. Box 227, Mankato, Minnesota 56002
Creative Education and Creative Paperbacks
are imprints of The Creative Company
www.thecreativecompany.us

Design by Ellen Huber
Production by Grant Gould
Art direction by Rita Marshall
Printed in the United States of America

Photographs by Alamy (Adrian Buck, PA Images, Yelizaveta Tomashevska, Wavebreak Media ltd, Donka Zheleva), Dreamstime (Konstantinos Moraitis), Getty (Stephen Simpson), iStockphoto (mladn61, stockstudioX, tampatra), Shutterstock (Africa Studio, Alaettin Y1LDIRIM, doomu, Lens Hitam, LittlePerfectStock, Joko SL, Stuart Monk, Jaroslav Pachy sr, Quality Master, sondem, Petr Student, Syda Productions)

Copyright © 2023 Creative Education, Creative Paperbacks
International copyright reserved in all countries.
No part of this book may be reproduced in any form
without written permission from the publisher.

ISBN 9781640264069 (library binding)
ISBN 9781628329391 (paperback)
ISBN 9781640005709 (eBook)

LCCN 2020907008

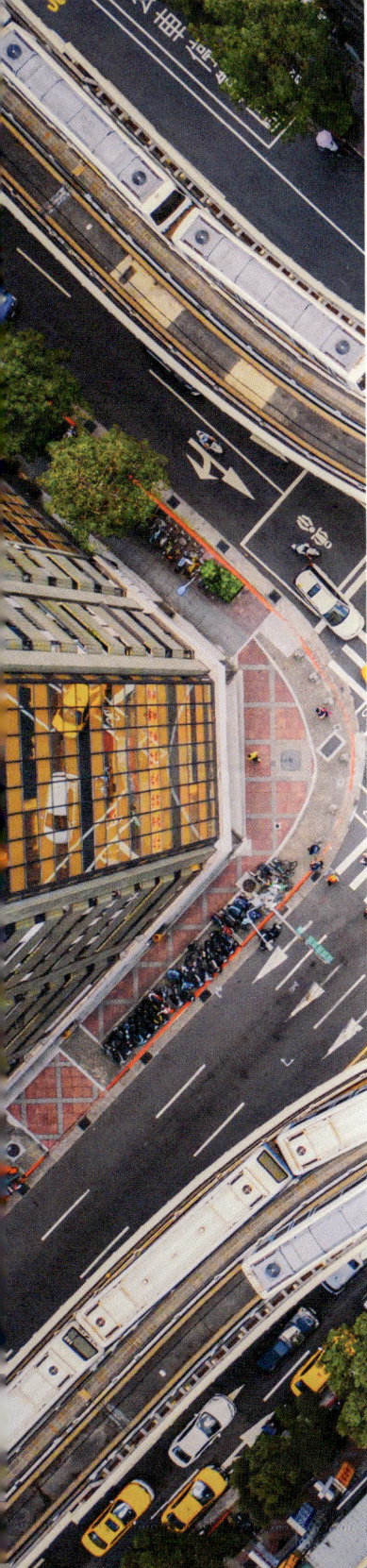

TABLE OF CONTENTS

Hello, Bus Drivers! 5

Place to Place 6

Big and Small 8

School Buses 10

City Buses 13

Safe on the Road 14

What Do Bus Drivers Do? 16

Thank You, Bus Drivers! 18

Picture a Bus Driver 20

Words to Know 22

Read More 23

Websites 23

Index 24

Hello, bus drivers!

Bus drivers take people from place to place.

They spend lots of time on the road.

Some bus drivers drive a small bus.

Others drive a big bus.

Bus drivers need special **training**.

School bus drivers take students to and from school. The driver puts out a stop sign. Other **vehicles** stop.

Many bus drivers work in cities. They go to **bus stops** or stations.

Bus drivers follow rules. They stay safe on the road.

They drive in rain, snow, and fog.

Bus drivers make many stops.

They follow a route. Riders get on and off. The bus driver helps them.

Thank you, bus drivers!

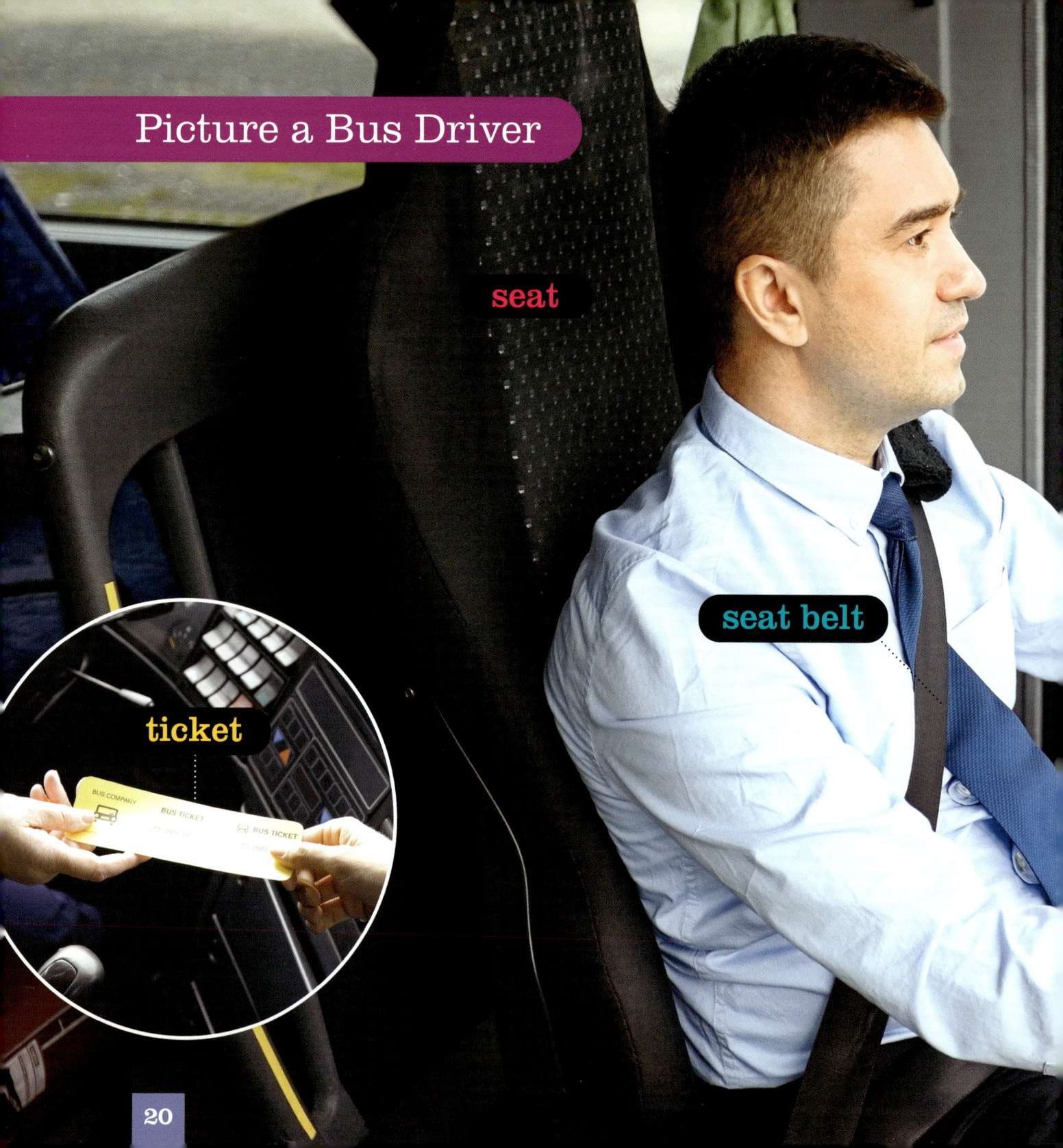

Words to Know

bus stops: places where buses stop to pick up or drop off people

route: a set path for traveling

training: something that makes a person get better or ready

vehicles: things that move people or things

Read More

Arnold, Quinn M. *School Buses*.
Mankato, Minn.: Creative Education, 2019.

Schuh, Mari. *Bus Drivers*.
Minneapolis: Bellwether Media, 2018.

Websites

Bus Coloring Pages
http://www.supercoloring.com/coloring-pages/transport/school-bus

Let's Ride the Bus
https://tpt.pbslearningmedia.org/resource/ket-earlychild-ss11/lets-ride-the-bus/

Note: Every effort has been made to ensure that the websites listed above are suitable for children, that they have educational value, and that they contain no inappropriate material. However, because of the nature of the Internet, it is impossible to guarantee that these sites will remain active indefinitely or that their contents will not be altered.

Index

jobs 6, 7, 10, 13, 17
people 6, 10, 17
routes 17
rules 14
safety 14
school 10
size 8, 9
stops 10, 13, 16
training 9
weather 15